KISS *of the*
SPIDER WOMAN

KISS *of the* SPIDER WOMAN

THE SCREENPLAY

LEONARD SCHRADER

Based on the novel by Manuel Puig

Introduction by David Weisman

FABER AND FABER
BOSTON & LONDON

Copyright © 1987 by Leonard Schrader

Based on the novel *Kiss of the Spider Woman* by Manuel Puig,
translated by Thomas Colchie. Copyright © 1978, 1979 by
Manuel Puig. Published by Alfred A. Knopf, Inc. Screenplay
published in the United States by Faber & Faber, Inc.,
50 Cross Street, Winchester, Massachusetts 01890.

Library of Congress Cataloging-in-Publication Data
Schrader, Leonard.
Kiss of the spider woman.
I. Puig, Manuel.   Beso de la mujer aràna.   English.
II. Title.
PN1997.K447   1987   791.43'72   87-6841
ISBN 0-571-12993-5 (pbk.)

INTRODUCTION

BY DAVID WEISMAN

I welcome this opportunity to introduce a screenplay that changed my life. Although screenwriter Leonard Schrader and I come from radically different backgrounds, we both arrived in Hollywood in the early seventies after extensive journeys abroad during the sixties. When we met we soon found that we shared similar views on independent filmmaking, and deep affinities for the cultures of Japan and South America.

Leonard left the intense Dutch-Calvinist life of Grand Rapids, Michigan, by accepting a teaching post at Kyoto University. He wound up living five years in Japan, and in some senses still does. Personal experiences there led to the writing of Sidney Pollock's film *The Yakuza*, and his younger brother Paul Schrader's film *Mishima*. Additionally, Len has written several strictly Japanese movies, including the prize-winning *Taiyo Nusunde Otoko* (*The Man Who Stole the Sun*). Before becoming immersed in Japan, Leonard did graduate studies in modern Latin American Literature at the Iowa Writers' Workshop. And by coincidence, while Len was in the midwest learning his craft under Jose Danosa and Borges himself, I was wandering South America on my own Candide-like adventure before discovering *my* second homeland—Brazil.

Leonard and I met making a film in Japan that unexpectedly became a blockbuster in that market. Encouraged by our first collaboration, we struggled to find a new project we could both believe in. About this time we saw several Brazilian films that were playing the arthouse circuit: Carlos Diegues' *Bye Bye Brasil*, *Dona Flor* (which introduced Sonia Braga to the world), and Hector Babenco's *Pixote*, among others. Clearly, something exciting was happening below the equator, so I decided to return to Brazil for the first time in thirteen years to investigate the possibilities. I arrived in Rio de Janeiro on Christmas day, 1981 — my Portuguese rusty, but still fluent. I had been given some subtle hints by Fabiano Canosa (of the Public Theater in New York, who championed Brazilian cinema in the United States) and by New Year's Day I managed to meet the Brazilian directors whose work Len and I had seen — a small but remarkably sophisticated circle of filmmakers, most of whom had emerged from the underground *cinema novo* movement of the sixties. I sensed that I had found my destiny. I would make the first really international Brazilian movie. My twenty-year-long familiarity with the language, culture, and sensibilities of Brazil was clearly the only asset I needed to build the bridge. Then, just as I began to look for the right project, Hector Babenco introduced me to the movie-obsessed world of author Manuel Puig and his exquisite novel *Kiss of the Spider Woman*. A stage play of Puig's cult bestseller was popular in Rio/Sao Paulo at the time, and Babenco sensed that it would make a wonderful film, if only he could persuade the reclusive novelist to grant the rights. Hector was in despair. Puig was disgusted by versions of his earlier works done by Latin American filmmakers, and staunchly refused to sell Babenco the rights — both were Argentines living in Brazil, and if Puig was skeptical about regional directors, another Argentine was out of the question.

As I listened to Hector bemoan his plight, I began to think out another approach. When Puig and I met, he immediately began to explain his concerns; gradually it became clear that all Manuel really wanted was reliable assurances of a quality screen adaptation — in English — a kind of "international passport" for his most cherished creation. He shrewdly understood that this was the way to attract two really fine international actors for Molina and Valentin. When he saw that I understood this as well, Manuel began to view the proposal in a whole new light. Eventually he gave his blessings and generous support to the film.

In retrospect I realize that the direction established during the process of acquiring the Puig rights was the first of three fundamental turning points in making *Kiss of the Spider Woman* a unique film. Unwittingly, I had taken the first step in evolving a hybrid

6

form of independent production. This would be the first time a South American film was made in English with American stars for the international market. And inevitably, the issue at the heart of each crucial juncture was the script.

When I returned to Los Angeles I asked Leonard Schrader to read Puig's novel. He was struck by its avant-garde mix of cool style and hot content. He considered Molina as rich a character as Falstaff or Hamlet. I was pleased that he shared my enthusiasm; it seemed as if we'd found the project we were looking for — the one we could believe in despite evidence that our beliefs would take us on a long road of sacrifice and humility.

In the beginning is the word; or, as Len puts it, black marks on white paper. Until you have a good script, nothing of substance can ever happen on a production. And if you have a script that is *really* good, other good things will happen.

The second critical juncture in the project's evolution was casting Molina and Valentin. Early on, Burt Lancaster had read Puig's novel and expressed a strong desire to play Molina — at the time, a mammoth risk for a star of his stature and age. Moreover, he was so taken with the challenge that he himself suggested he would go to Brazil and work for nothing, if necessary, to get the film made. With Lancaster's enthusiasm as an inspiration, Len worked a year for almost no money to write a script he was proud of, one he felt would convey the power and emotion of Puig's story on the screen. Leonard is not the kind of writer who dashes out a script haphazardly; in fact, he generally will not write the first sentence until he pretty much has the last one in his mind.

Waiting for Leonard to complete his draft drove poor Hector mad. He never believed we would find financing in the United States — no South American production ever had before. All Babenco really wanted to achieve in America was to nail down the participation of Burt Lancaster, an actor he deeply admired and who had often worked with foreign directors. Waiting a year for a writer to perfect a script was not part of Babenco's spontaneous and emotion-charged style. Moreover, he was extremely insecure about making a film in English, a language he had not yet mastered. Luckily, this factor plus his anxieties about Latino integrity caused us to gravitate to Raul Julia as the ideal Valentin to Burt Lancaster's

Molina. But even that charismatic cast and a proposed budget under $3 million could not persuade a single studio or independent to finance the film. One after another, the reactions were the same: "A fascinating and brilliant script; we're sure it will make a great film — but unfortunately it's not for us. Good luck and if you do get it made please let us be the first to see it."

What we had in the eyes of any potential money source was a marketing nightmare. Typical Marketing Analysis one-liner: "A QUEER AND A COMMIE TRAPPED IN A PRISON CELL DISCUSS OLD MOVIES AND LEARN TO LOVE." Only Los Angeles attorney Peter Dekom shared my dogged determination to pursue each financing lead to the end, but nothing could overcome the perception of marketing nightmare — except the quality of the script, when it was finished the way Leonard wanted it.

In mid-March of 1983, shortly after Raul Julia's agent Jeff Hunter confirmed that Raul would do Valentin, I got a strange call from another agent in the same office, Gene Parseghian, who praised the script as one of the best he'd read in years and asked if I had ever considered William Hurt.

I was baffled by the question, assuming he meant William Hurt for the role of Valentin, to which his agency had just committed Raul Julia. Sensing my confusion, Parseghian clarified that he was suggesting Hurt for the role of Molina. I must admit I was even more baffled, because the icon of Burt Lancaster as Molina had dominated my mind for over a year. Parseghian understood and gently requested that if for any reason Lancaster did not do the part, would we please consider William Hurt. I agreed.

For me, it was a remarkable experience to have a script that had such a powerful effect on virtually all who read it — except the money people. But perhaps the ultimate irony was that Burt Lancaster, who we had hoped so much would like the script, never really felt comfortable with it. Then, in late May '83, we learned he was to undergo major heart surgery. Now, for health reasons, he could no longer contemplate the strain of making a movie in Brazil that year.

With Lancaster out of the picture, Babenco was once again in despair. He was determined to make his movie before the Puig rights-option expired, and had long since abandoned any hope of finding money in the States. He returned to Sao Paulo with his page-by-page Portuguese translation of Len's script to raise the *cruzeiros* to make the film with Brazilian actors.

The following week, I called Gene Parseghian in New York and asked if he was still serious about William Hurt. He responded affirmatively and immediately pouched the script to Hurt in London, where he'd just completed *Gorky Park*. Three days later, Parseghian called and quietly said, "David, William Hurt loves Leonard Schrader's script and will do *Kiss of the Spider Woman* subject to a meeting with Hector Babenco and a screening of his previous film."

The power of black marks on white paper.

It was understandably difficult for a director like Babenco to assimilate the notion of William Hurt as Molina. Virtually since the project was born, Burt Lancaster had been Hector's fantasy of Molina. Now, before he could forget his dream of Lancaster, he was informed that the script had had a profound effect on William Hurt, an artist whose work Hector scarely knew, but whose craft and power as a screen actor were undeniable. Len and I were thrilled, and our optimism persuaded Hector to fly north once more to see what would happen.

In early July we all met in New York and decided to make the film together: Bill, Raul, Hector, Len, and myself. We all worked without compensation; our salaries became "deferred equity" investments in the film. The cash needed for production (including the "Nazi Movie" insert film) in Brazil and post-production in Los Angeles was raised from a group of investors in Sao Paulo and my friends Jane Holzer and Michael Maiello in New York, plus a small advance against Brazilian rights from Embrafilme in Rio de Janeiro. We had no completion bond, nor any real guarantee that the film would ever be finished or distributed. Those who invested agreed to recoup simultaneously with the deferred equity participants, the deal language reciting the mutual risks and sacrifice required to make the film without compromise to anyone but ourselves.

On the plane, Hector ran into Sonia Braga and spontaneously invited her to play the cameo role of Marta, Valentin's girlfriend. By September, when we began rehearsals, Len had completed the final shooting script, including modifications of the Molina char-

9

William Hurt, Hector Babenco (director), and Raul Julia

acter for William Hurt and certain structural adjustments, such as
the decision to make the "Nazi Movie" the only complete movie
tale Molina would tell. The novel contains five movie tales; in one
preliminary shooting script Molina told portions of both the "Nazi
Movie" and the original *Cat People*, while another draft opened
with the conclusion of a Mexican melodrama. Sonia was also cast
as diva Leni La Maison, the chanteuse in the Nazi propaganda film-
within-the-film, and the enigmatic Spider Woman, linking the three
women characters in the story. Manuel Puig came to Sao Paulo
from Rio often during pre-production, generously providing details
for the "Nazi Movie."

We shot for a total of ninety-seven days, from October '83 through
February '84. As grueling as it may have seemed, the real heartache

was yet to come. Post-production was done in Los Angeles on a shoestring that kept getting longer and longer. Leonard had left Sao Paulo shortly after shooting began to join his brother Paul in the making of *Mishima* in Tokyo. Hector and I had big problems in the editing room. In his eyes, the film was finished at a length and pace I found unbearable. Through the Los Angeles summer we remained deadlocked until Len resurfaced, exhausted from the ordeal of the *Mishima* shoot, but nonetheless with a vital fresh eye. Hector then returned to Brazil to supervise the musical score while Len and I began to hone down the picture. In Sao Paulo, Hector discovered he had lymphoma cancer. This tragedy had a profound effect on the completion of the film. Len and I had to supervise the balance of post-production, involving continual refining of the picture cut and extensive ADR (voice-dubbing) of the actors, while Bob Dawson created the complex main titles and color desaturation for the "Nazi Movie." Hector was able to be with us during the first mix at Sound One Studio in New York during November '84, but not for the final re-cut mix at Fantasy Studios in Berkeley the following April.

Leonard's return from Tokyo in mid-July was the film's final turning point. He saw the film in his mind's eye, as only the screenwriter can. Despite physical exhaustion, he could instantly analyze the problems of pacing and cutting by a very blunt standard: "Slow doesn't mean profound, and art is never boring — because if it's boring, it's not art." The script design required holding audience attention for an inordinate span before sinking the plot hook — to achieve this, performances and pacing were crucial.

From the independent production worldview that Leonard Schrader and I shared before my visit to Brazil in 1981, four Academy Award nominations — Best Picture, Best Actor, Best Director, Best Screenplay Adaptation — and a Best Actor Oscar were beyond the realm of possibility. Starting with William Hurt's triumph at the 1985 Cannes Film Festival, through the record-breaking openings of *Kiss of the Spider Woman* that summer, critics' lists, Golden Globes, right up to the "Big Night" itself on March 24th, 1986 — it was a dream voyage that began with Len's black marks on white paper.

KISS *of the*
SPIDER WOMAN

The screen is BLACK. *We hear a "woman's"* VOICE.

VOICE OF MOLINA: She, uh. Well, something a little strange,
that's what you notice, that she's not a woman like all the
others.
(*pause*)
She seems all wrapped up in herself. Lost in a world she
carries deep inside her. But surrounded by a world of
luxury.
(FADE TO:)

INT. PRISON CELL — NIGHT

We PAN *a stark cell and discover a woman's touch — glamor
magazines, earrings, clothesline, pin-ups of Lana Turner and Rita
Hayworth.*

VOICE OF MOLINA: A sumptuous boudoir. Her bed all quilted
satin. Chiffon drapes. From her window you can see the
Eiffel Tower.
(*pause*)
Suddenly her maid brings in a gift-wrapped box, a token
from an admirer. She's a cabaret star, of the highest rank.
She opens the box, it's a diamond bracelet, but she sends it
back.
(*pause*)

William Hurt

Men are really at her feet. She's known a few; but not the
one she's been waiting for all her life—a real man.
(*The camera finds the* PRISONER *who is speaking.*
He is LUIS MOLINA, *41, his red-tinted hair no longer hiding the*
gray. He has the seasoned face of a man who has seen it all, and
been hurt by most of it.)

MOLINA: Her maid has prepared her a foam bath. The star takes
a towel and wraps it around her hair like a turban. Her
fingernails painted a rosy peach, she unfastens her taffeta
night gown and lets it slide smoothly down her thighs to
the tile floor.
(*Molina, playing the role, wraps a red towel around his head and*
sashays toward the other bunk.)

MOLINA: Her skin glistens, her petite ankle slips into the
perfumed water, then her sensuous legs, until finally her
whole body is caressed with foam.
(*The* CELL-MATE *glances over his shoulder. He is* VALENTIN
ARREGUI, *34, his arms marked by torture. He has has the intense*
look of a man who has been hurt in more ways than one.)

VALENTIN: I told you. — No erotic descriptions.
(*Molina hides his delight at having evoked a response.*)

MOLINA: Whatever, but she's a ravishing woman, do you know
what I mean? I mean the most ravishing woman in the
world.

VALENTIN: Yeah, sure.

MOLINA: She really is — perfect figure, classical features, but with
these big green eyes.
(*We drift into the* MOVIE *he describes. A glamorous* STAR *in a*
lavish bathtub caresses her skin with foam. Valentin's voice
wrenches us back to the cell.)

VALENTIN: They're black.

MOLINA: I'm the one who saw the movie, but if that' s what you
want — big black eyes.
(*resumes*)
Kind eyes, tender eyes, but beware. They can see
everything.
(*pause*)
There's nothing you can hide from them.

(*Another* MOVIE *flash. The Star steps from the foamy water and gazes into a mirror with big sad eyes.*)

MOLINA: No matter how lonely she may be, she keeps men at a distance.

VALENTIN: (*laughs*) She's probably got bad breath or something.

MOLINA: If you're going to crack jokes about a film I happen to be fond of, there's no reason to go on.
(*Molina glares at him. Valentin turns away, too weak to care one way or the other.*)

VALENTIN: Alright, alright. Go ahead.

MOLINA: Suddenly we're in Paris! Troops are marching right underneath the Arc de Triomphe. Really handsome soldiers, and the French girls are applauding as they pass by.
(*pause*)
Then we're on this typical Parisian back-street, dead end, sort of looking up a hill.
(*Another flash.* TWO FRENCHMEN *with yarmulkes unload a truck in the dark. The images resemble a slapdash Nazi propaganda film.*)

MOLINA: And these really weird-looking Frenchmen, not the typical ones with the berets, are unloading a truck. It's wartime, of course, and the boxes contain contraband delicacies. Like canned meat . . . the best cheeses . . . peaches in syrup—

VALENTIN: (*sitting up*) Don't talk about food.

MOLINA: Not to mention the hams, and the pates—

VALENTIN: I'm serious. No food and no naked women.
(*Valentin struggles to the shit-bucket in the corner and, exhausted, leans against the wall as he urinates.*)

MOLINA: You still feeling dizzy?

VALENTIN: It's my back.

MOLINA: You've been bleeding again. Look at your shirt, it's all wet.

VALENTIN: It's just sweat. I had another fever break.

MOLINA: What do you think so far?
(*pause*)
Isn't it fabulous?

VALENTIN: It helps pass the time.

Raul Julia

(*Valentin hobbles toward his bunk. His shirtback is streaked with old bloodstains.*)

MOLINA: Does that mean you like it?

VALENTIN: Doesn't help any great cause, but I guess it's alright.

MOLINA: Blessed Mary, is that all you can talk about? You must've studied Political Philosophies in school.

VALENTIN: The phrase is Political *Science*, and the answer is no, I studied Journalism.

MOLINA: Ah! So you *can* appreciate a good story.

VALENTIN: And easily spot a cheap one.

MOLINA: Well, I know it's nothing terribly intellectual like you must be used to. It's just a romance, but it's so beautiful. (*pause*)
Now. Suddenly this military convoy rushes forward.
(CUT TO:)

EXT. PARIS BACK-STREET — NIGHT (NAZI MOVIE)

Spotlights hit the Frenchmen unloading the truck. German TROOPS *grab them. A handsome* LIEUTENANT *shoves one against the truck.*

VOICE OF MOLINA: Marvelous German soldiers catch those weird smugglers in the act and arrest them all.
(*A small truck lurks in the shadows.*)

VOICE OF MOLINA: But watching nearby is this small truck, with these two French thugs from the Resistance who are spying on the Germans. — This hulking Clubfoot and his half-deaf Flunky.
(CUT TO:)

INT. CELL — NIGHT

Valentin sits up on his bunk.

VALENTIN: Wait a minute. Those weird guys the Germans arrested?

MOLINA: Yes?

VALENTIN: What do you mean, they didn't look French?

20

MOLINA: They didn't look French. They looked, uh, Turkish. I'm not sure, they had like these caps on their heads—like these, like these, uh . . . Turkish. Like fezzes.

VALENTIN: Those caps are yarmulkes. Can't you see this is a fucking anti-Semitic film?

MOLINA: Oh, come on!

VALENTIN: Wait. This must've been a German movie, right?

MOLINA: I don't know, it was from years ago.—Look. I don't explain my movies. It just ruins the emotion.

VALENTIN: This must've been a Nazi propaganda film done during the war.

MOLINA: I don't know, that's just the background. This is where the important part begins, the part about the lovers. It's divine.

(CUT TO:)

INT. PARIS CABARET—NIGHT (NAZI MOVIE)

Deco doors swing open. Elegant waiters move along dimly-lit tables.

VOICE OF MOLINA: Every night the chic set flocks to this exclusive club—with lovers at every table, spies in every corner. And the top officers of the German High Command.

(*pause*)

One of them is Werner. Werner, so distant, so divine. And the Chief of Counter-Intelligence for all France.

(*pause*)

And Michelle with her angel face, the cigarette girl who really is working for the—well, you'll see.

(*Michelle leaves the table of the handsome blond Werner. Musical* FANFARE. *Dancing couples sit and applaud.*)

VOICE OF MOLINA: And then, the moment they're all waiting for.

(CUT TO:)

INT. CELL—NIGHT

Molina opens his clothesline towels like a stage curtain and strikes a grandiose pose.

MOLINA: Stepping into the spotlight is that legendary star, that ravishing chanteuse—Leni La Maison!
(CUT TO:)

INT. CABARET—NIGHT (NAZI MOVIE)

LENI *turns to the crowd in a deco pose and, singing, glides and swirls among the hushed tables. Werner can't take his eyes off her. Michelle hurries backstage and picks up the phone.*

MICHELLE: Yes?
CLUBFOOT: (*on phone*) Did you get the map?
MICHELLE: No, there was no time.
CLUBFOOT: (*hanging up*) Just get it. Nothing else matters. Vive La France.
   (*Leni, still singing, passes Werner's table with a haughty glance and concludes with a flourish, then sees him gazing at her. Wild applause.*)
VOICE OF MOLINA: Werner's eyes begin to burn into her soul. Eyes like the claws of an eagle—inescapable.
   (*Leni clutches her pounding heart and dashes away from his piercing eyes.*)
   (CUT TO:)

INT. CELL—NIGHT

Valentin muffles his scornful laughter. Molina, miffed, plunks down on his bunk.

MOLINA: What are you laughing at?
   (*more laughter*)
   Well, it must be something.
   (*Valentin stares straight at Molina.*)
VALENTIN: At you.
   (*looks away*)
   And me.
   (*Molina blows out his candle. The two men sit in silence on opposite ends of the dark cell.*)
   (CUT TO:)

EXT. PRISON CORRIDOR — NIGHT

TWO GUARDS *drag an old* HOODED PRISONER *into a cell across the courtyard. His shirt is covered with bloodstains.*

(CUT TO:)

INT. CELL — NIGHT

Valentin watches through the food slot in the door. Molina wakes up and rubs his eyes.

MOLINA: What's going on?
VALENTIN: (*tense whisper*) Quiet! They're bringing in someone new.
MOLINA: What time is it anyway?
VALENTIN: He's really bleeding.
MOLINA: Is it a political prisoner?
VALENTIN: They don't treat you like that for stealing bananas.
MOLINA: You know him?
(*Valentin, deeply disturbed, says nothing.*)
(CUT TO:)

INT. PRISON CORRIDOR — DAWN

GUARDS *conduct the morning bedcheck. Prisoners bark out their names.*

VALENTIN: Valentin Arregui!
MOLINA: Luis Molina!
(*Valentin strains to see the hooded prisoner across the courtyard. The guard shoves him in his cell.*)
(CUT TO:)

INT. CELL — DAY

Molina finishes shaving and offers the razor.

MOLINA: Do you want to shave?
VALENTIN: (*turns away*) Shit.

MOLINA: Well, I didn't mean your legs.

(*Valentin looks out the crack in the metal wall plates.*)

MOLINA: *What* is the matter?

VALENTIN: I don't understand why they stopped my
interrogation. It's been almost a week.

MOLINA: Why couldn't they give me that handsome leading
blond man to keep me company — instead of you.

VALENTIN: What the hell are you talking about?

MOLINA: Afraid to talk about sex?

VALENTIN: You really wanna know, Molina? I find you boring.

MOLINA: Darling, you don't know page one. You know I'm a
faggot? Well, congratulations. You know I corrupted a
minor? Well, that's even on TV, film at eleven.

VALENTIN: You really like those Nazi blonds, don't you?

MOLINA: Well, no, you see I detest politics but I'm *mad* about the
leading man. He's so romantic.

(*pause*)

Should I be shot for that?

VALENTIN: Your Nazis are about as romantic as the fucking
warden and his torture room.

MOLINA: I can imagine.

VALENTIN: (*hard*) No. You can't.

(*Valentin stares into his eyes. Molina, chagrined, looks away.*)

(CUT TO:)

INT. CELL — NIGHT

*Valentin, unable to sleep, climbs up to the barred window and stares at
the city lights in the dark. Molina, drowsy, sits up on his bunk.*

MOLINA: You can't sleep?

(*pause*)

Mind if I tell my picture?

(*Valentin stares out the window.*)

MOLINA: After the show, Leni changes into a satin evening-gown
that makes her look heavenly. Firm breasts. Thin waist.
Smooth hips.

VALENTIN: Is this propaganda or porno?

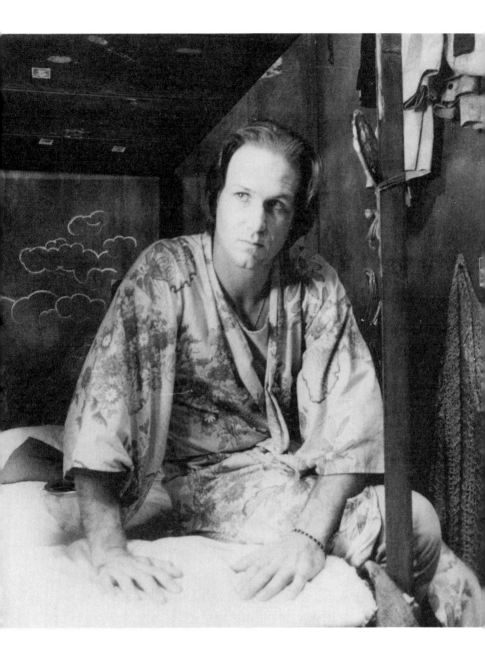

MOLINA: Just listen, you'll see.

(CUT TO:)

INT. CABARET DRESSING ROOM — NIGHT (NAZI MOVIE)

KNOCK *on the door. Michelle, upset, enters Leni's ornate dressing room.*

MICHELLE: Excuse me. Leni.

LENI: What is it, Michelle?

MICHELLE: (*near tears*) Leni, I'm a traitor. A traitor to France.

LENI: What do you mean?

MICHELLE: I'm going to have a baby. ·But the father is a young Lieutenant of the Occupation Army.

LENI: Is that so? My poor Michelle.

MICHELLE: But he loves me. And wants to get married as soon as he can get permission.

LENI: I really can't understand. How could you fall in love with an enemy of our France?

MICHELLE: Love has no country, Leni.

(*pause*)

But there's something else you don't know. I'm working for the Resist—

(*Another* KNOCK. *Michelle gasps.*)

LENI: Come in!

(*A* MESSENGER *enters with a bouquet of flowers. The two women sigh with relief.*)

MESSENGER: For you, Madame.

(CUT TO:)

INT. CELL — NIGHT

Valentin shakes his head in disgust.

VALENTIN: How can you remember all this crap? You must be making it up.

MOLINA: No, I'm not, I swear. Well, I embroider a little, so you can see it the way I did.

VALENTIN: God help me.

MOLINA: You atheists never stop talking about God.

VALENTIN: And you gays never face facts. Fantasies are no escape.

MOLINA: If you've got the keys to that door, I will gladly follow. Otherwise I'll escape in my own way, thank you.

VALENTIN: Then your life is as trivial as your movies. —I'm going to sleep.

MOLINA: Tell the truth, Valentin. Who do you identify with the most—the Clubfoot patriot or the handsome Werner?

VALENTIN: Who do *you* identify with?

MOLINA: Oh, the singer. She's the star. I'm always the heroine.

(CUT TO:)

INT. CELL—DAY

Sunlight streams through the bars. Molina slices an avocado and offers it to Valentin.

MOLINA: Have some, it's delicious.

VALENTIN: No thanks.

MOLINA: What's wrong, you don't like it?

VALENTIN: Sure I like it, but no thanks.

MOLINA: Well, then go ahead and have some. It's a long time till lunch.

VALENTIN: Can't afford to get spoiled.

MOLINA: Do you really think eating this avocado will make you spoiled and weak? Enjoy what life offers you.

VALENTIN: What life "offers" me is the struggle. When you're dedicated to that, pleasure becomes secondary.

MOLINA: Does your girlfriend think the same thing?

VALENTIN: (*suspicious*) How do you know I have a girl?

MOLINA: (*shrugs*) It's the normal thing. Does she avoid pleasure too?

VALENTIN: She knows what really counts. That the most important thing is serving a cause that is noble.

MOLINA: What kind of cause is that, one that doesn't let you eat an avocado?

27

VALENTIN: (*turns away*) Molina, you would never understand.
MOLINA: Well, I understand one thing. I offer you half of my
    precious avocado and you throw it back in my face!
VALENTIN: Don't act like that. You sound just like a —
MOLINA: Like a what? Say it. Like a woman, you mean.
    (*Valentin shrugs yes.*)
MOLINA: What's wrong with being like a woman? Why do only
    women get to be sensitive? Why not a man, a dog, or a
    faggot? If more men acted like women, there wouldn't be so
    much violence. — Like that!
    (*Molina points at the welts on Valentin's face.*)
    (CUT TO:)

EXT. PRISON CORRIDOR — DAY

A GUARD *walks down the corridor and unlocks their door.*

VALENTIN (O.S.): Maybe you have a point, a flimsy one but
    still —
MOLINA (O.S.): Oh nice! Maybe I have a point!
    (CUT TO:)

INT. CELL — DAY

The fat guard steps into their cell.

GUARD: Molina, today's yer lucky day. The Warden wanna talk
    to ya.
    (*Molina is led away.*)
    (CUT TO:)

INT. CELL — NIGHT

*Molina mends a shirt with needle and thread. Valentin cleans his teeth
with a damp rag.*

VALENTIN: Why did the Warden want to see you?

MOLINA: My lawyer called. Parole seems out of the question.
(*sighs*)
For a while, at least.

VALENTIN: How'd he treat you, the Warden?

MOLINA: Like a faggot, same as always.
(*lights out*)
Oh, no. Shit.
(*Curfew* BUZZER. *Molina lights a candle and places it near the photo of his mother.*)

MOLINA: He told me something else. My mother's not doing too well. She has high blood-pressure, and her heart is kind of weak.

VALENTIN: People can go on forever like that.

MOLINA: (*melancholy*) Sure, but not if you upset them. Can you imagine the shame of having a son in prison?
(*pause*)
And the reason.

VALENTIN: Go to sleep, you'll feel better.

MOLINA: No, only one thing can help.

VALENTIN: (*grudgingly*) Sure, man. Go ahead.

MOLINA: Man! Is there a man in here? Don't let him go!
(*looks under bed*)
Did he get away?

VALENTIN: (*exasperated smile*) Okay, cut the crap and tell your movie.
(*Molina, beaming, spins his web of romantic intrigue.*)

MOLINA: And now, waiting in the moonlight behind the cabaret is Werner's limousine.
(CUT TO:)

EXT. CABARET BACK DOOR — NIGHT (NAZI MOVIE)

Werner watches Leni say goodbye to Michelle.

VOICE OF MOLINA: Werner's eyes are locked on the backstage exit. "La sortie des artistes." He signals his chauffeur to open the door for her. Maybe because Leni sees a chance to help Michelle, or maybe because Leni wants to know what

kind of a man is hidden inside this enemy invader—she
decides to join him for the evening.
(*Leni descends the stairs. Werner offers his hand.*)
WERNER: Madame.
(*With a haughty glance, she enters his limousine.*)
(CUT TO:)

INT. NIGHTCLUB—NIGHT (NAZI MOVIE)

Leni and Werner lift champagne glasses. Their eyes meet.

WERNER: (*clicks glasses*) To a great artiste.
(CUT TO:)

EXT. PARIS STREET—NIGHT (NAZI MOVIE)

Michelle walks along a dark neighborhood street.

VOICE OF MOLINA: Michelle hurries to meet her secret love. But
dark forces have already decided the fate of this sweet girl.
This girl from the French Resistance in love with a German
Lieutenant. Because . . .
(*The Clubfoot and his Flunky watch her hurry past their parked
truck.*)
CLUBFOOT: Her time is up.
FLUNKY: (*grips hearing aid*) What?
(*Michelle approaches an elegant apartment building.*)
VOICE OF MOLINA: Because . . . love is a luxury a spy cannot
afford.
(*She calls up to the balcony.*)
MICHELLE: Hanschen!
(*The German Lieutenant appears on the balcony, smiles and tosses
down his key. It lands in the street.*
*Michelle stoops down to pick it up. Suddenly the truck hurtles
toward her at full speed. Turning in horror, she sees the Clubfoot
at the wheel.*
*The truck races into the night, leaving Michelle sprawled across
the dark pavement.*)
(CUT TO:)

INT. CELL — NIGHT

Valentin is deep in thought. Molina approaches and snaps his fingers.

MOLINA: Valentin, are you listening?
(*pause*)
How can you leave me chattering to myself like some silly parrot?
VALENTIN: Strange. When Michelle was killed, I — it was chilling.
(*Molina, touched by the compliment, sits on the floor beside his bunk.*)
MOLINA: It's just a movie, Valentin. One of Mother's many stories.
VALENTIN: Yeah, but I keep thinking about — someone I know.
MOLINA: Your girlfriend. Tell me about her. My lips are sealed.
VALENTIN: It's just that I'm so helpless in here, with no way to protect her.
MOLINA: So you have a heart after all.
VALENTIN: Mm.
MOLINA: Write to her. Tell her to stop taking chances.
(*Valentin snaps out of his reverie.*)
VALENTIN: If you think like that, you'll never change anything in this world.
MOLINA: (*amused*) Now look who's living a fantasy.
(*Valentin angrily lifts his shirt, displaying the torture welts on his torso.*)
VALENTIN: You call this a fantasy?
MOLINA: — I'm so sorry.
VALENTIN: Some day the struggle will be won.
MOLINA: Don't worry, Valentin. You'll have your day, I'm sure.
(CUT TO:)

EXT. PRISON CORRIDOR — DAY

Both men stand outside their door for morning bed-check.

VALENTIN: Valentin Arregui.
MOLINA: Luis Molina.
(CUT TO:)

INT. CELL — DAY

Molina leans on his bunk, humming Leni's song. Valentin paces for exercise. Two tin plates are pushed through the food slot in the door.

VALENTIN: Great. I'm starving. —Here.

MOLINA: No, you take this one. It has twice as much.

VALENTIN: Sure, because those bastards want us to fight over it. Take it.

MOLINA: No, you need it more than I do. Please, please, to build your strength.

VALENTIN: Don't argue. Take it.

(Molina reluctantly accepts the larger portion.)

MOLINA: *(snide)* May I have a spoon?

(Valentin obliges)

Thanks.

(Valentin sits on his bunk and eats the black beans, then notices Molina toying with his food.)

VALENTIN: What's the matter? Afraid of getting fat?

MOLINA: No.

VALENTIN: This glue is not so bad today.

(Molina hesitantly swallows another spoonful.)

MOLINA: Valentin.

(pause)

When I said you should write your girlfriend, I also meant you should tell her you love her. It's so nice to get a letter from someone you love.

VALENTIN: Are you crazy? A letter would be like denouncing her to them. The only reason I'm still alive is because they want information from me. And if anyone tries to save me, they'd hide my arrest by killing me on the spot.

MOLINA: *(upset)* Valentin, please don't say things like that.

VALENTIN: The same thing could be happening to her. Right now.

MOLINA: *(melancholy)* You love her very much, don't you. Love should always come first.

VALENTIN: That's great.

(turns away)

Now I'd like to eat in peace.

MOLINA: Don't worry, I won't disturb you.
(*Molina bursts into muffled sobs.*)
VALENTIN: (*annoyed*) What is it now?
MOLINA: (*weepy moans*) It's my mother. She must really be in bad
shape or she'd come visit me with groceries. This happened
once before.
VALENTIN: (*cold*) Sorry to hear that.
(*Molina moans more. Valentin keeps eating and tries to ignore
him. Molina moans louder, then says:*)
MOLINA: Yeah, well, I told you she was sick, but of course you
weren't paying any attention.
(*pause*)
But that's not what I'm crying about.
VALENTIN: (*very annoyed*) So what is it, for Chrissake?
MOLINA: (*wipes tears*) Because it's so beautiful when lovers are
together for a lifetime. Why is it so impossible?
VALENTIN: You gotta be crazy, crying about something like that.
MOLINA: I will cry about whatever I want to.
(*stops crying*)
Valentin, do you think you're the only one who's suffered?
You think it's easy to find a real man? One who's humble,
and yet has dignity?
(*pause*)
How many years have I been searching? How many nights?
How many faces filled with scorn and deceit?
(CUT TO:)

EXT. STORE WINDOW — DAY (FLASHBACK)

*The window contains two mannequins dressed as bride and groom.
Molina meticulously adjusts the fluffy bridal gown.*

VOICE OF MOLINA: You know, working as a window dresser,
enjoyable as it is, sometimes at the end of the day you
wonder what it's all about. And you feel kind of empty
inside.
(*pause*)
Then, one night. . . .
(CUT TO:)

INT. RESTAURANT — NIGHT (FLASHBACK)

Molina takes a table with two effeminate friends. One is black. The other is GRETA, *31, babbling with chit-chat.*

GRETA: It's something new she just invented herself. She calls it
  La Chika-Chaka and she goes chika-chaka, chika-chaka.
  And she's an overnight sensation, the next day she's in *all*
  the newspapers, and her husband becomes so jealous because
  he thinks —
    (Molina's eyes are riveted on GABRIEL, *34, a handsome waiter in
    a white tunic.)*
GABRIEL: Good evening, gentlemen. Would you care for the
  daily special? Or would you like to order a la carte?
MOLINA: I haven't decided yet.
    (Gabriel offers a menu and leaves.)
VOICE OF MOLINA: My heart was pounding . . . so afraid that I
  would be hurt once again.
    (CUT TO:)

INT. RESTAURANT — NIGHT (FLASHBACK)

Molina sits alone, impeccably dressed, immaculately groomed.

GABRIEL: Are you ready for me, sir?
MOLINA: What do you suggest?
GABRIEL: Perhaps the lasagna and antipasto.
MOLINA: Don't you think the lasagna might be fattening?
GABRIEL: Then perhaps the steak and onion soup.
MOLINA: *(returning the menu)* Sounds wonderful.
    *(Gabriel goes to place the order. Molina can't take his eyes off
    him.)*
VOICE OF MOLINA: His white tunic, the way he moved, his sad
  smile. Everything seemed so perfect, like in the movies.
    (CUT TO:)

INT. RESTAURANT — NIGHT (FLASHBACK)

*The restaurant is closed. Gabriel mops the floor. The only customer is
Molina, still in his chair, waiting.*

VOICE OF MOLINA: You have no idea how much trouble I went through, month after month, just to get him to go for a walk. But little by little I made him see I respected him.
(CUT TO:)

INT. CELL — NIGHT

Molina sits on the floor, hugging his knees.

MOLINA: Anyway, after more than a year, we finally became friends.
VALENTIN: Jesus, did it take another year to get him in the sack?
MOLINA: Are you out of your mind? Nothing at all happened. Ever!
VALENTIN: You gotta be kidding.
MOLINA: Don't you know anything at all? He's straight. He's married. I said to him, let's do it just once. But he never wanted to.
VALENTIN: I don't believe this. Here I am, staying up all night, thinking about your boyfriend.
(*pause*)
Sounds like a real bind, Molina. All you can do is take it like a man.
MOLINA: I take it like a woman. Always. That's why I want a husband who's the boss.
(*Molina stretches across the floor toward Valentin's bunk. Valentin awkwardly changes the subject.*)
VALENTIN: Uh, did you ever meet his wife?
MOLINA: No, but when they were on the verge of splitting up— God, such illusions I had.
VALENTIN: Like what?
MOLINA: That he might come home to live with me, with my mother and me. And I would take care of him and help him lose that sadness of his forever.
(CUT TO:)

EXT. BAR DISTRICT — NIGHT (FLASHBACK)

Molina and Gabriel stroll up the narrow street. Most of the garish bars are dark. Male and female HOOKERS stand in shadowy doorways.

35

GABRIEL: (shrugs) That's life, Molina.

MOLINA: No, it's a shame. With your looks and charm, you should work in a chic restaurant in a luxury hotel. Making three times what you get in that stinkhole.

GABRIEL: It's not so easy.

MOLINA: I know someone who works in a big hotel on the Coast. He could talk to the manager and presto, a new life.

GABRIEL: And be what, a busboy in a snob joint? I'd make less money than now.

MOLINA: I could help you with a loan. With your poise, you'd be a waiter in six months.

GABRIEL: I don't know.

MOLINA: Of course you do. And in a year, a maitre d'. In a tuxedo! You could pay me back in no time.

GABRIEL: Maybe. Anyway, I appreciate your offer. I'll think about it.

(leaving)

I gotta get my bus, I'm gonna be late. See you tomorrow, Molina.

MOLINA: Goodnight, Gabriel. Kiss the children for me.

(Molina watches the bus leave, then heads back down the dark street toward the male hookers. A teenage BOY asks for a light. Molina responds and they walk off together.)

VOICE OF MOLINA: And then it's over . . . again . . . my dreams disappear . . . into the darkness. And I wake up alone.

(CUT TO:)

INT. CELL — NIGHT

Molina, stretched out on the floor, looks up at Valentin.

MOLINA: Waiting as always. Waiting and waiting. Waiting and waiting and waiting.

VALENTIN: Waiting for what?

MOLINA: A man. A real man. But that can't happen because a real man, what he wants is a real woman.

VALENTIN: (stands up) Can I ask you a question? What is a real man in your terms?

MOLINA: Well, to be marvelous looking and strong. Without making any fuss about it. And walking very tall. Like my waiter.

VALENTIN: He just gives you that impression, but inside it's another story. In this society, without power behind you, no one walks tall.

MOLINA: Don't be jealous.

VALENTIN: Don't be stupid.

MOLINA: You see how you react? There's just no talking about a guy with another guy without getting into a fuss.

VALENTIN: (*hard*) Look, just keep it on a certain level, okay? Or let's not talk at all.

MOLINA: Okay, you tell me what a real man is.

VALENTIN: (*caught off guard*) I don't know.

MOLINA: Sure you do. Go ahead, tell me.

VALENTIN: Well, not taking any crap from anyone, not even the powers-that-be. That's not the most important thing; what really makes a man has to do with not humiliating anybody. It's not letting the people around you feel degraded.

MOLINA: That sounds like a saint.

VALENTIN: Forget it.

(*Molina suddenly grabs his stomach and doubles over, groaning in pain.*)

VALENTIN: What's wrong?

MOLINA: (*drops to floor*) — My stomach.

VALENTIN: Maybe it's your appendix?

MOLINA: No, I had mine out.

(*grimacing*)

God, it hurts, it hurts!

VALENTIN: You feel like throwing up?

MOLINA: No, it's below there. It's in my guts.

(*Valentin pulls Molina to his feet and helps him hobble to his bunk.*)

VALENTIN: The food didn't do anything to me.

MOLINA: (*lays down*) I don't know, maybe it's my ulcer.

(*writhing in pain*)

I — I don't like this!

VALENTIN: Why don't you go on with your movie?

MOLINA: God, I never felt a pain like this.
VALENTIN: Go ahead and tell it.
(CUT TO:)

EXT. LENI'S APARTMENT — NIGHT (NAZI MOVIE)

Leni stands at her window, waving goodbye to Werner in his limousine.

VOICE OF MOLINA: Leni lingers at the window, so sad, so alone,
so afraid that she will fall in love.
*(Suddenly a hand reaches from the shadows and muffles her
scream. It's the half-deaf Flunky.)*
(CUT TO:)

INT. LENI'S APARTMENT — NIGHT (NAZI MOVIE)

*The Flunky flings Leni onto a sofa. She sees the Clubfoot in her
armchair.*

CLUBFOOT: Tonight the invaders murdered your friend Michelle.
LENI: *(shocked)* No.
CLUBFOOT: You must complete her mission and find the secret
map to the German arsenal. The Chief of Counter-
Intelligence is in love with you.
LENI: I could never get involved with such a thing.
CLUBFOOT: *(approaching)* Nonsense, nothing could be safer. Do
you love France?
LENI: Of course I do.
CLUBFOOT: That Kraut can't keep his hands off you. Next time
he touches you like this —
(fondling her)
— and like this, think of your country. And get the map.
*(Leni has grasped a statuette of "Justice." She hammers his skull
and dashes out the door. The Clubfoot tumbles to the carpet and
shouts at his Flunky.)*
CLUBFOOT: Stop her, you idiot!
(CUT TO:)

39

Sonia Braga

EXT. PARIS STREET — NIGHT (NAZI MOVIE)

Leni runs across dark cobblestones, turns a corner and sees a taxi in the distance.

LENI: Taxi! Taxi!
    (*The bleeding Clubfoot lumbers around the corner.*)
VOICE OF MOLINA: Leni, desperate, runs along this dark empty
    street. The furious Clubfoot hobbles after her, when
    suddenly —
    (CUT TO:)

INT. CELL — NIGHT

Molina, hunched over the edge of his bed, clutches his stomach and whispers:

MOLINA: — this girl is finished.
VALENTIN: What girl?
MOLINA: Me, stupid.
(*Molina, passing out, slumps onto the floor. Valentin pounds the cell door.*)
VALENTIN: Guard! *Guard!*
(CUT TO:)

INT. PRISON INFIRMARY — NIGHT

Molina sleeps on an infirmary cot.

(CUT TO:)

INT. CELL — NIGHT

Valentin looks under Molina's bunk and finds his crucifix neck-chain. He places the gold chain on Molina's pillow.

(CUT TO:)

INT. PRISON INFIRMARY — DAY

Molina, in bed, reaches for his missing crucifix and looks up at the prison DOCTOR.

DOCTOR: You're strong enough to go back to your cell. Your diarrhea will stop tomorrow. Till then, no food. Only water. Clean water. If you can find it.
MOLINA: Doctor, I need to see the Warden. Right away.
DOCTOR: (*leaving*) That's what they all say.
(CUT TO:)

INT. CELL — NIGHT

Valentin does pushups on the floor. Molina pages through glamor magazines on his bunk.

VALENTIN: I don't understand how you can pass out from an ulcer.
MOLINA: I'm no spring chicken, darling. I'm getting dizzy just looking at these pictures.
(Molina sighs for attention. Valentin says nothing.)
MOLINA: God, wouldn't it be wonderful if you told me a movie for a change. One that I haven't seen.
VALENTIN: I don't remember any.
MOLINA: Don't be like that. Come on, tell me one.
(pause)
Please.
VALENTIN: Don't be such a cry-baby.
MOLINA: Valentin. Have you ever loved someone you didn't *want* to love?
VALENTIN: *(wary)* What do you mean?
MOLINA: Leni didn't want to fall in love with Werner, but what could she do? She steps through his doorway like a goddess. Her slim graceful figure trembles at the sight of Werner descending the marble staircase. Their eyes meet. Leni says —
(CUT TO:)

INT. CHATEAU — NIGHT (NAZI MOVIE)

Werner descends his marble stairs. Leni stands beside the BUTLER in the vestibule.

LENI: My best friend has been killed. I need a place to stay.
WERNER: *(to Butler)* Prepare the guest room.
LENI: This music is magical. I feel like I'm floating on air.
(Wagnerian music fills the baroque chateau. Werner leads Leni inside.)
VOICE OF MOLINA: But her heart is saying, Oh Werner, you seem like a god, but your tears —
(CUT TO:)

INT. CELL — NIGHT

Molina savors his sad reverie.

MOLINA: —your tears are proof you have the feelings of a man.

VALENTIN: Quiet! I can't hear.

(*Valentin peers through the wall plate and* SEES *two Guards returning the Hooded Prisoner in blood-stained underpants. His skin is covered with welts and burns.*

Valentin bangs the door with his metal cup.)

VALENTIN: Murderers! Fascist murderers. Fascist murderers!

(*More prisoners join the protest. The guards use clubs to crush the outbreak.*

Valentin sees a guard's shoes facing his cell. Suddenly a stream of urine splashes onto Valentin. SOUND *of guards laughing.*)

VALENTIN: Motherfucker. Motherfucker!

MOLINA: I'll clean it up.

(*Valentin, furious, spins around and hurls his metal cup at Molina's head. Molina ducks. Valentin stalks forward.*)

VALENTIN: You son of a bitch! They're killing one of my brothers and what am I doing? Listening to your fucking Nazi movie!

(*Molina clutches his ragdoll to his chest.*)

VALENTIN: Don't you know what the Nazis did to people— Jews, Marxists, Catholics? Homosexuals!

MOLINA: Of course I know. What do you take me for, an even dumber broad than I am?

(*Valentin grabs Molina and hurls him headfirst across the cell, then fires the doll at his face. Molina cowers on the floor.*

Valentin clenches his fist and approaches.)

VALENTIN: You don't know shit. You wouldn't know reality if it was stuck up your ass.

MOLINA: (*terrified*) Why should I think about reality in a stinkhole like this? Why should I get more depressed than I already am?

(*Molina shrinks back into the corner. Valentin, seething, kneels down and rips off Molina's earrings.*)

VALENTIN: You're worse than I thought. You just use these movies to jerk yourself off.

MOLINA: (*bursts into tears*) If you don't stop, I will never speak to you again.

VALENTIN: Stop crying! You sound just like an old woman.

MOLINA: (*sobbing*) That's what I am, that's what I am.

(*Molina looks down, whimpering. Valentin violently wrenches apart Molina's knees.*)

VALENTIN: What's this between your legs? Huh? Tell me, "lady"!

MOLINA: It's an accident. If I had the courage, I'd cut it off.

(*Molina struggles to regain his dignity. Valentin moves in for the kill.*)

VALENTIN: You'd still be a man! A man in prison, just like the faggots the Nazis shoved in the ovens.

MOLINA: (*pleading*) Don't. Don't look at me like that.

(*Molina, sobbing, looks up at the barred window.*)

(CUT TO:)

INT. COURTROOM — DAY (FLASHBACK)

Molina stands beside his LAWYER, *facing the massive oak desk. The* JUDGE *glowers down at him.*

JUDGE: . . . Luis Alberto Molina. You shall endure the full weight of the law and not one day less. You will be confined without chance of parole for a period of not less than eight years.

(*Molina turns from the Judge to gaze forlornly at his* MOTHER. *She pulls a handkerchief from her purse. As their eyes meet, she smiles warmly through her tears.*)

VOICE OF MOLINA: Poor Mama. Her eyes full of tears as if someone had died. A life full of humiliation and then the humiliation of a son steeped in vice, but she never gave me that black look. Her heart broken by too much suffering, too much forgiving. Because of me she could die.

(CUT TO:)

INT. CELL — DAY

Molina's red eyes are stark and determined.

MOLINA: If he ever says one unkind word about her, I'll strangle the son of a bitch. Him and his filthy words and his piss-ass revolution.
(*Lightning flashes through the barred window.*)
(CUT TO:)

INT. CELL — NIGHT

Two plates are shoved through the food slot. Molina, still angry, plops one on Valentin's bunk and goes to eat by the window. Lightning flashes.
Suddenly Valentin clutches his stomach and groans in pain. Molina rushes to his side.

VALENTIN: My stomach. It's like a bomb exploding.
MOLINA: The same thing I had.
VALENTIN: (*grimacing*) I think it's the food.
MOLINA: You gotta go to the Infirmary right now. — Guard!
(*Molina hurries to the door. Valentin lunges forward and grabs him.*)
VALENTIN: No! Wait. Stop.
MOLINA: Why?
VALENTIN: I'm a political prisoner.
MOLINA: Don't be ridiculous. This is no time for your damn discipline.
VALENTIN: Get away from the door.
MOLINA: They gave me a shot, and I'm better already.
VALENTIN: Are you crazy? That's just what they want. They get me hooked on those shots, and I'll tell them everything.
MOLINA: What else can we do?
(*Valentin, groaning, returns to his bunk and mutters:*)
VALENTIN: Leave me alone.
(*Molina thinks, then gets a scarf and says:*)
MOLINA: What about my movie? It might help you forget the pain.
(CUT TO:)

EXT. CHATEAU — NIGHT (NAZI MOVIE)

Leni and Werner slowly waltz among billowing white curtains.

VOICE OF MOLINA: Later that night, on the moonlit veranda, Leni feels so safe, so secure in Werner's arms.
(*music stops*)
Even when the phonograph stops, they continue dancing . . . dancing.
(CUT TO:)

INT. CELL — NIGHT

Molina dances with the scarf as if his empty arms held Werner.

MOLINA: To the music of the evening breezes, whooh, whoooh.
(*Molina sees Valentin shivering in his sleep, drenched with sweat. He kneels down and wipes Valentin's fevered forehead with the scarf.*)
VALENTIN: (*asleep*) Marta . . . Marta.
(*opens eyes*)
. . . who are you?
MOLINA: It's okay. Try to rest.
(*Valentin closes his weary eyes. Molina tenderly adjusts the blanket.*)

INT. CELL — NIGHT

Both men are eating. Molina watches Valentin reading a letter.

MOLINA: You shouldn't eat this garbage while you're sick.
VALENTIN: (*keeps eating*) I have to get my strength back.
MOLINA: It'll only make you worse.
VALENTIN: Tastes like dog piss.
MOLINA: (*shakes his head*) My poor little Valentina.
VALENTIN: Don't call me Valentina. I'm not a woman.
MOLINA: (*leans forward*) Well, I've never seen proof to the contrary.
VALENTIN: And you never will.
MOLINA: Now, the Clubfoot told—
(*Valentin grimaces in disgust.*)
MOLINA: You'll like this part, wait and see.
(CUT TO:)

INT. WERNER'S BEDROOM — DAY (NAZI MOVIE)

Leni wakes in a lavish antique bed, reaches for Werner and discovers he is gone.

VOICE OF MOLINA: The Clubfoot told Leni that her sweet lover was ordering the execution of her countrymen everyday. But she refused to believe it. She only wanted to live this love, to feel his touch, to hear his voice.
(*The phone rings. Leni eavesdrops on Werner.*)
WERNER'S VOICE: It's a difficult decision.
CALLER'S VOICE: Ja, Herr Commandant.
(CUT TO:)

INT. WERNER'S STUDY — DAY (NAZI MOVIE)

Werner, in uniform, stands at a desk piled with documents.

CALLER'S VOICE: We captured ten of them. They're all French, but their activities prove they are enemies of the people.
WERNER: They call themselves patriots, but in fact they are common criminals.
(CUT TO:)

INT. WERNER'S BEDROOM — DAY (NAZI MOVIE)

Leni sits up in shock.

WERNER'S VOICE: Let the execution take place at dawn.
(CUT TO:)

INT. CELL — NIGHT

Molina looks at his fingers.

MOLINA: Her fingers tremble with the agony of betraying the man she loves.
(*Valentin suddenly curls up with pain.*)

48

VALENTIN: It's like a nail in my gut.

(*pause*)

That's better. Do me a favor and stop all this crap about beautiful women in tears.

(*Molina goes to the corner for coconut shells and returns, clutching them to his chest under his robe.*)

MOLINA: Leni's heart was beating so fast that her swelling breasts leapt out of her low-cut gown. Like luscious hors d'oeuvres on a silver platter.

(*Valentin chokes with laughter.*)

VALENTIN: Don't make me laugh. It hurts.

(*Molina opens his robe, revealing the coconut-shell breasts.*)

MOLINA: Here, have a nice juicy tit. Have another. The best places serve them in pairs.

(*Valentin laughs out loud. Suddenly, his eyes snap open in pain. Trying to sit up, he clutches his pants and points to the shit-bucket.*)

VALENTIN: The bucket! Quick!

(*Molina dashes to the bucket. Valentin struggles to his feet and tugs his zipper. Diarrhea fills his trousers. Valentin collapses on the floor, covering his face in shame.*)

VALENTIN: Oh, no.

MOLINA: Christ, what a smell.

VALENTIN: (*groaning*) I'm sorry. You don't know how much it hurts.

MOLINA: Let it all out. It can't smell any worse than it already does.

VALENTIN: God, I can't stand this.

(*Valentin trembles on the floor. Molina pulls the sheet from his own bed and grabs some rags.*)

MOLINA: You've been through worse. Much worse.

VALENTIN: I'm so ashamed.

MOLINA: Aren't you the one always saying take it like a man? So what's this business about being embarrassed?

VALENTIN: I can't stand it. I can't stand myself like this.

(*Valentin lifts his hand to hide his tears. Molina kneels down with maternal concern.*)

MOLINA: Take off your pants. Cover yourself with this. Why do you always have to pick on yourself so much?

(*Molina tosses the soiled trousers and underpants beside the bucket, then grabs the rags.*)

MOLINA: Wipe yourself off.

VALENTIN: No, it's yours.

MOLINA: No, it's ours. Wipe yourself. There's a little more here, and here.

(*Valentin struggles to remove the glop from his buttocks. Molina wipes the brown liquid from his ankles.*

Despondent, Valentin gives up. Molina, taking over, cleans his thighs and buttocks like a mother cleaning a child.)

VALENTIN: (*turning away*) Jesus, aren't you disgusted?

MOLINA: No, it breaks my heart to see you like this. There, almost finished. Good. Now take off your shirt.

VALENTIN: No, it's alright.

MOLINA: The shirt-tails are soiled. Please.

(*Valentin removes his shirt. Tossing it, Molina feels a letter in the pocket and keeps it.*)

MOLINA: Okay, now try and stand up.

(*Molina, tenderly insistent, helps him to his feet and puts the bedsheet around his shoulders.*)

VALENTIN: No, it'll stink.

MOLINA: My weekly shower is tomorrow. I'll have it all clean by noon. There we go. All wrapped up like a little papoose.

(*Molina wraps the bedsheet around him like a toga and helps him crawl back in bed.*)

VALENTIN: It doesn't disgust you?

MOLINA: Lie down. Don't want you to catch a chill. What a shame I have no talcum left. Are you comfortable now?

VALENTIN: Yes, but I'm so cold.

MOLINA: I'll make you a nice hot cup of tea.

(*Valentin, deeply touched, watches him pour a cup.*)

MOLINA: This will work wonders.

(*hands cup*)

It's hot, you'll burn yourself.

(*Valentin takes a sip.*)

VALENTIN: You're very kind, honestly, I don't know what to say.

MOLINA: Don't burn yourself.

(*Molina finishes cleaning the floor, then pulls out the hidden letter.*)

MOLINA: Oh, uh, this fell out of your shirt.

VALENTIN: Go ahead, read it. I know you've been curious.

MOLINA: No, I only read love letters. I don't want to know anything about your politics.

VALENTIN: It's from my girlfriend. Her name is Lydia.

MOLINA: — What about Marta?

VALENTIN: (*bolts upright*) How do you know about Marta?

MOLINA: You mumbled her name in your sleep.

VALENTIN: (*worried*) What else did I mumble?

MOLINA: Nothing.

VALENTIN: The letter's from Lydia. She's my girlfriend in the movement.

(*Molina opens the pages and scans the letter.*)

MOLINA: Her handwriting is like a child's.

VALENTIN: — She hasn't had much of an education.

(*Valentin lays back down with a sigh.*)

VALENTIN: I'm going to tell you the truth. During torture, whenever I felt close to death, it was Marta I would think about, and she would save me. My whole body ached to hold her.

MOLINA: What's she like?

VALENTIN: She's upper-class. Pure bourgeoisie. She's got everything. Money, looks, education, freedom. I'm such a hypocrite. Just like all those class-conscious pigs.

(*pause*)

I must admit it was convenient, a safe place to stay when I was forced to hide. Until one day I had to tell her about my other life.

(CUT TO:)

INT. HIGH-RISE APARTMENT — DAY (FLASHBACK)

MARTA, *29, puts out a cigarette and listens.*

VOICE OF VALENTIN: She just listened in silence like she knew already. Then she asked me to leave the movement. But

51

how could I do nothing when my friends were disappearing every day? I sensed that she was right but I had no choice. So once again I didn't know what to say.

(*Marta steps onto the balcony and looks at the city. Her strong eyes brim with tears. Valentin approaches.*)

VALENTIN: Things are what they are. I'll be back in a few days. Same as always.

MARTA: I can't take it any more. Always waiting, watching the phone. Always alone.

(*Valentin brushes back her long black hair and kisses her cheek. She makes no response. He turns to leave.*)
MARTA: (*fights back tears*) Valentin. If you leave, don't come back. Please, don't come back.
(*Valentin hesitates, then leaves.*)
(CUT TO:)

INT. TRAIN — DAY (FLASHBACK)

Valentin, deep in thought, stares out the train window at the passing slums.

VOICE OF VALENTIN: I no longer believed in violence, but I had to do something. As a journalist, I was always hearing about the illegal arrests and secret torture, then leaking this information abroad.
(CUT TO:)

EXT. TRAIN STATION — DAY (FLASHBACK)

The train pulls into a station. Valentin steps onto the platform.

VOICE OF VALENTIN: My assignment was to meet one of the last surviving members of the original movement. His code name was Americo. He needed my passport to leave the country.
(*Valentin approaches an old man.* AMERICO, *62, walks with a cane toward a railing. Valentin stops beside him.*)
VALENTIN: Are you all right?
AMERICO: A little tired.
VALENTIN: You should have left long ago, Doctor Americo.
AMERICO: (*points down*) This is where I'm needed.
VALENTIN: I keep wondering if it's all worth it — when nothing really changes.
(*Valentin tugs the passport from his pocket and slides it along the railing.*)
VALENTIN: Well, good luck. Here's your passport. Take care of yourself.

53

AMERICO: Thank you.

(*Americo walks away. Valentin stays at the railing.*)

VOICE OF VALENTIN: He had accomplished almost nothing, but I was glad I could help him.

(CUT TO:)

EXT. STATION ENTRANCE — DAY (FLASHBACK)

Reaching street level, Valentin steps off the escalator and enters the turnstyle. Suddenly THREE PLAIN-CLOTHES AGENTS *surround him with guns.*

Their burly leader, PEDRO, *44, black, spins Valentin around and jams an automatic pistol in the back of his head.*

PEDRO: Freeze! Stop!

(*frisks him*)

Open your legs.

(*handcuffs him*)

Move!

(*Pedro shoves Valentin toward a black car.*)

VOICE OF MOLINA: What happened to Marta?

(CUT TO:)

INT. CELL — NIGHT

Valentin, tormented, lays on his bunk in the sheet. Molina sits at the foot of the bed.

VALENTIN: I don't know anything for sure. Except that I'll never see her again.

MOLINA: Don't say that.

VALENTIN: (*writhing*) I don't deserve to die in this cell. I only confessed some code names they already knew. I can't stand being a martyr, it infuriates me. I don't *want* to be a martyr.

(*deeply depressed*)

My whole life . . . a mistake.

MOLINA: No.

(*Valentin, fighting despair, extends his hand.*)

54

VALENTIN: Give me your hand.
(*Molina grips his hand tightly. Valentin whispers:*)
VALENTIN: I don't want to die, Molina. I don't want to die.
Don't let me die.
MOLINA: (*grips tighter*) Of course not.
(CUT TO:)

INT. WARDEN'S OFFICE — DAY

The WARDEN, *60, gray-haired in a business suit, leans forward at his large desk.*

WARDEN: You look thin, Molina, what's the matter?
MOLINA: It's nothing, sir. I was sick, but I'm better now.
WARDEN: So stop trembling. There's nothing to be afraid of.
(*pause*)
Arregui doesn't suspect anything, does he?
MOLINA: No, sir.
WARDEN: What has he told you?
MOLINA: Uhh. Nothing yet. He, uh, I feel I should proceed very
cautiously.
(*Stepping from the adjoining bathroom is Pedro, the Secret Agent who arrested Valentin. Wearing a three-piece suit, he adjusts his tie and measures Molina with ice-cold eyes.*)
PEDRO: Molina, you are lying. What are you hiding?
MOLINA: Nothing.
(*to Warden*)
How can you accuse me when I almost died for you? He
insisted I eat the bowl with the poison.
(*The Warden pushes back from his desk and rolls around front in a wheelchair.*)
WARDEN: Why? You made a mistake there.
MOLINA: One plate had twice as much as the other one, so he
insisted I eat the larger portion. Sir, you told me the
poisoned food would be in a new tin plate, but they loaded
it up so much I had no choice. I had to eat it myself, or he
would've become suspicious.

WARDEN: Poor Molina. I'm sorry for the mix-up. I commend you. Sit down here. Please.

(*Molina takes a seat. The Warden wheels closer, treating him like a child.*)

WARDEN: Your mother's feeling much better since she learned you may be paroled.

MOLINA: Really?

WARDEN: Of course. So stop crying. You should be pleased.

MOLINA: It's from happiness, sir.

(*Pedro takes the chair beside Molina and says curtly:*)

PEDRO: What did Valentin say about his cadre?

MOLINA: (*puzzled*) His what?

PEDRO: His group — who they are, where they meet.

MOLINA: Nothing, sir. He is very sick. If he has anymore poison, I don't know *what* will happen.

PEDRO: His girlfriend, what'd he say about her?

MOLINA: He says personal things are secondary to revolution, he thinks everything else is trash, so I think he's warming up to talking about it.

(*The Warden hands him a cup of coffee.*)

MOLINA: For me? Thank you.

PEDRO: What did he say about the new prisoner? The one across the hall.

MOLINA: The one who's all messed up? He said that no crime justifies that kind of punishment.

(*takes a sip*)

This coffee really hits the spot.

PEDRO: Did he tell you his name?

MOLINA: (*puzzled*) Of course, sir. It's Valentin Arregui.

PEDRO: No, you idiot! The name of the new prisoner.

MOLINA: (*frightened*) Of course not. He's always wearing a hood.

(*Pedro, furious, glances at the Warden.*)

PEDRO: Who put a hood on him?

WARDEN: (*worried*) It's routine. He's political.

PEDRO: How do you expect him to talk if he can't even see the bastard's face?

WARDEN: It won't happen again.

(*Pedro looks at his "female" prisoner. He's not sure if this "actress" is really naive — or just pretending.*)

PEDRO: Molina, we gotta know everything they're planning.
(*pause*)
As soon as he sees that new prisoner's face, he'll spill his
guts. Remember every damn word he says.
MOLINA: Yes, sir.
PEDRO: The quicker he talks, the quicker you get out. Now get
back to work.
(*Molina stands up to leave, then hesitates.*)
MOLINA: Uh, Warden, one more thing. He heard the guard say
my mother was coming. And I told him that, uh, she
always brings me a bag full of groceries. I don't want him
to get suspicious.
WARDEN: Okay, dictate what she brings.
MOLINA: To you, sir?
WARDEN: Yes, to me! And make it quick. I'm busy.
MOLINA: Um. Two roast chickens in butter, egg salad, canned
peaches, condensed milk. Two boxes of tea—one regular,
one camomile. A jar of pickled herring, four bars of toilet
soap. What else?
(*Pedro, disgusted, watches the Warden write it down. Molina
nervously taps his teeth, watching from the corner of his eye,
pushing them to the limit.*)
MOLINA: Blessed Mary, my mind's a blank. Let me think. Rye
bread. Sugar, I need. Uhh.
(*The Warden, exasperated, eyes the ceiling.*)
(CUT TO:)

INT. CELL—DAY

*Valentin struggles to sit up in bed. Molina, victorious, unpacks two
bags of groceries.*

MOLINA: Roast chickens! Canned peaches! Cheddar cheese! Rye
bread!
VALENTIN: What happened?
MOLINA: Look at this. Two roast chickens, *two*! How about that.
Just watch how fast you get better now.
VALENTIN: Your mother came.

57

MOLINA: Yes! Tea, sugar, and—
(proud chuckle)
cigarettes.
VALENTIN: That's great. How is she?
MOLINA: Oh, she's much better, thank you. And look at all she
brought me. I mean *us*.
VALENTIN: Well, really that's all meant for you.
MOLINA: No, you have to stop eating that damn prison chow,
and you'll feel better in no time.
VALENTIN: You think so?
MOLINA: You're damn right I do. Starting today a new life
begins. Oh, I took a chance and left the sheets out to dry,
and no one walked away with them. So tonight we both
have clean sheets.
(He tosses the sheets. Valentin catches them and smiles.)
VALENTIN: Nice going.
MOLINA: (lights the burner) Let me get this started and presto, in a
few minutes you'll be licking your fingers. I expect you to
eat all of those chickens, *both* of them.
VALENTIN: But what about you? I'm not gonna let you just sit
around and drool.
MOLINA: No, I've gotta keep an eye on my girlish figure. At
least what's left of it.
(Valentin reaches for the peaches. Molina slaps his hand.)
MOLINA: Not yet, that's for dessert.

TIME CUT:

Spread across the floor is a picnic blanket of leftovers. Valentin relaxes
with a cigarette. Molina stretches.

MOLINA: Would you like some more peaches?
VALENTIN: No thanks. I'm stuffed.
(rubs stomach)
Good food, good cigarette. I don't remember when I felt so
good. There's only one thing missing.
MOLINA: Christ! And I thought I was supposed to be the one
who's the degenerate around here.

VALENTIN: (*laughs*) No, I mean a good movie.

MOLINA: Of course! Jeez, why didn't I think of that?

VALENTIN: Your Nazi movie, how does it end?

MOLINA: I thought you hated it.

VALENTIN: Yeah, but I'm curious to see how it turns out.

MOLINA: (*stands up*) Well, let's see.

    (CUT TO:)

INT. WERNER'S DINING ROOM — NIGHT (NAZI MOVIE)

Leni and Werner sit at a magnificent table.

VOICE OF MOLINA: They are dining at the majestic table in
    Werner's chateau. As Werner begins to notice Leni's cold
    distance, she suddenly—
    (*Leni stands up with a crystal goblet.* INSERT: *In the cell, Molina*
    flings his tin cup at the wall. In the chateau, his tin cup turns into
    her crystal goblet.)

VOICE OF MOLINA: —impulsively, hurls her wine glass across the
    room and says—

LENI: I refuse to love a man who is the butcher of my country.

WERNER: (*stands up*) Oh, my love. Come with me and you'll
    understand.
    (CUT TO:)

INT. CELL — DAY

Molina and Valentin sit side-by-side against the wall. In the fading
daylight, Molina spins his delicate web.

MOLINA: Werner takes her to this government archive, filled
    with photos and documents about famine throughout the
    world.
    (CUT TO:)

INT. PROJECTION ROOM — DAY (NAZI MOVIE)

Slides show the tragedy of famine. Leni wipes a teardrop.

VOICE OF MOLINA: He shows her how the elite create false
   shortages to enslave the masses. Leni is deeply moved and
   begins to see things through Werner's eyes.
   (CUT TO:)

EXT. GOVERNMENT ARCHIVE — DAY (NAZI MOVIE)

Leni and Werner walk arm-in-arm along a corridor of columns.

VOICE OF MOLINA: From that moment on, Leni understood
   Werner's mission. To liberate humanity from injustice and
   domination. As they leave the baroque archive, Leni feels

the anguish in her heart being transformed back to her previous admiration, but this time with the depth of a love reborn.

(*Leni stops on the balustrade and looks into his eyes.*)

LENI: My love, how could I ever have doubted you.

(CUT TO:)

INT. CELL — NIGHT

In the darkened cell Molina quietly says:

MOLINA: She begs him to forgive her and promises to help ensnare his enemies.

(CUT TO:)

INT. CAR — NIGHT (NAZI MOVIE)

The Flunky drives an old sedan with Leni in the backseat.

VOICE OF MOLINA: She arranges this secret meeting with the head of the Resistance by telling him that she will give the map — remember the map? — only to him.

(CUT TO:)

EXT. CASTLE — NIGHT (NAZI MOVIE)

The sedan stops beside a dark castle. Leni runs up the stone steps and enters an underground tunnel. The Flunky waits at the entrance.

(CUT TO:)

INT. CASTLE — NIGHT (NAZI MOVIE)

Leni enters an underground chamber and sees the Resistance LEADER in the shadows.

LENI: (*offers map*) I believe this is what you want.

LEADER: Yes, well done. So often I was tempted to steal it from him myself. But some things are best done by a woman. A woman who betrays the man she loves.

(*The Leader steps from the shadows with a lecherous grin.*)

LEADER: And there is something else I have wanted almost as much as the map.

LENI: What?

(*Taking the map, the Leader backs Leni against the wall and nuzzles her neck.*)

LEADER: You know very well. I've prepared a lavish banquet for two.

LENI: I'm not hungry.

LEADER: I am. For you.

(*He paws her. Leni, struggling, spots a steak knife on the banquet table. Pretending to submit, she maneuvers him sideways and grabs the knife.*

Kissing him, she plunges the blade into his back. The Leader moans and topples to the floor.

Leni grabs the map and dashes into the dark tunnel.)

(CUT TO:)

EXT. CASTLE—NIGHT (NAZI MOVIE)

Rushing outside, Leni is grabbed by the Flunky. She elbows his throat and starts down the stone stairs.

He pulls a handgun and aims at her but, suddenly, is shot in the chest and drops to the ground.

Werner stands at the foot of the stairway with a smoking pistol. Leni, smiling, rushes into his embrace and kisses him.

The dying Flunky raises his gun and fires. Leni slumps back and dies in Werner's arms.

VOICE OF MOLINA: Werner hears her sing. She sings like never before. She sings of her eternal love for him and—

(CUT TO:)

INT. CELL—NIGHT

They sit side-by-side in the dark. Valentin is wrapped in his blanket. Molina is rapt in his web.

MOLINA: —begs him not to cry, because her sacrifice was not in vain.
(*sighs*)
The End.
(*pause*)
What did you think?

VALENTIN: (*shrugs*) You told it well. Next time tell one I like.

MOLINA: Come off it, the love story was divine. Forget about the rest. It's so perfect when Leni—
(*corridor noise*)
What's going on?
(*Valentin jumps up*)
What is it?
(*Valentin peers through the wall plate and SEES two guards dragging the Hooded Prisoner to his cell. He has no hood.*)

VALENTIN: (*stunned*) That guy is Americo.

MOLINA: Who?

VALENTIN: The man with my passport.
(*looks down*)
They don't know he's here.

MOLINA: Who doesn't know?
(*Valentin, depressed, turns to the wall.*)

MOLINA: Please, Valentin. Maybe I can help.
(*Valentin says nothing.*)
(CUT TO:)

EXT. PRISON COURTYARD — DAY

A prison WORK CREW *cleans out Americo's empty cell. They toss his bloody shirt in a trash can.*

(CUT TO:)

INT. CELL — DAY

Molina watches through the wall plate, then hears Valentin waking up.

MOLINA: Good morning. Did you sleep well?

VALENTIN: (*glances down*) Turn the other way, will you?

64

MOLINA: Why?

VALENTIN: Because you'll laugh.

MOLINA: At what?

VALENTIN: Something on any healthy man, that's all.

MOLINA: A hard-on. Well, that *is* healthy.

(*turns away*)

Should I close my eyes too?

(*Valentin grins and wraps a towel around his waist.*)

VALENTIN: Hey, I missed breakfast. Why didn't you wake me?

MOLINA: I told the guard not to bring anything as long as our food holds out.

VALENTIN: Dammit, Molina, stop running my life for me.

(*Molina nods an apology. Valentin moves toward the crack in the wall plate.*)

MOLINA: They already took him away. I didn't want to wake you. The water's almost hot if you want some tea.

(*Valentin stares at dead Americo's cell. Molina unwraps some baked goods.*)

MOLINA: Have some cake.

VALENTIN: You eat it.

MOLINA: (*offers cake*) Come on, let me spoil you a little bit.

VALENTIN: (*turns, glares*) Back off, Molina.

MOLINA: It's not my fault they killed your friend.

VALENTIN: Shut up!

(*slaps cake*)

You damn faggot!

(CUT TO:)

EXT. PRISON CORRIDOR — DAY

Two guards escort Molina across the courtyard and open his cell door. He carries two new bags of groceries.

(CUT TO:)

INT. CELL — DAY

Molina puts down the bags and pulls out a red heart-shaped box of candy.

MOLINA: Look at the wonderful things Mama brought me. And there's a special treat. Assorted bonbons.
(*Valentin watches in silence from his bunk, his hands folded around his knee. Molina sits near him with the candy box.*)
MOLINA: What's the matter? You don't like candy?
VALENTIN: About this morning . . . about my temper, I'm really sorry.
MOLINA: Oh, nonsense.
VALENTIN: It wasn't even you I was mad at.
(*pause*)
But I've been thinking. Maybe I *am* mad at you.
MOLINA: Why?
VALENTIN: Because you're so kind. I don't want to feel obligated to treat you the same way.
MOLINA: (*sing-song*) "Unable to take, unable to give."
(*Molina opens the candy box and slides it toward Valentin.*)
VOICE OF MOLINA: Every day he opens up more and more with me.
(NOTE: *We leave and return to the candy in the cell as Molina recalls his latest meeting with the Warden and Pedro.*)
(CUT TO:)

EXT. PRISON ROOFTOP — DAY

Molina faces them on the prison roof.

MOLINA: (*continues*) Just give me a few more days. I'm sure he'll talk.
PEDRO: If he don't, he'll be interrogated again. And thoroughly this time.
MOLINA: But he's too weak to be tortured. If he drops dead, we all lose out.
(CUT TO:)

INT. CELL — DUSK

Valentin sits on the floor beside the half-empty candy box.

VALENTIN: I can't take someone being nice to me without asking anything in return.

MOLINA: Well, if I'm nice to you, it's because I want your friendship and, why not say it? . . . your affection.
(*offers cigarette*)
The same way I try to be nice to my mother who's never harmed anyone, and who accepts me for what I am and loves me. It's like a gift from heaven, and the only thing that keeps me going, the only thing.
(*lights cigarette*)
And you too are a very good person.
(*Valentin, embarrassed, moves to the wall and smokes the cigarette.*)

MOLINA: Very selfless and devoted, risking your life for your ideals, ready to die even in here for what you believe in. Am I embarrassing you?

VALENTIN: (*shrugs*) No.
(CUT TO:)

EXT. PRISON ROOFTOP — DAY

Molina turns to the Warden.

MOLINA: Well, sir, there might be a way to speed this up. I'm not sure but I'm—it's just a hunch.

WARDEN: (*exasperated*) Say it straight, Molina.

MOLINA: You know inmates, sir. When a cell-mate leaves, they feel all sentimental and helpless. Well, he's gotten a bit attached to me, so if he thought that I was being released, he's bound to open up and talk. Get a few things off his chest.

WARDEN: (*to Pedro*) What do you think?
(CUT TO:)

INT. CELL — NIGHT

Valentin still leans against the wall with his cigarette. Molina watches from the bunk.

MOLINA: So that's why I respect you and like you, and hope that you feel the same way about me. So I want us always to be friends.

VALENTIN: Sure.

MOLINA: The reason I wanted to get this in the open is because I may be leaving, since I just heard from the Warden that I may be paroled soon.

VALENTIN: — When?

(CUT TO:)

EXT. PRISON ROOFTOP — DAY

Pedro removes his suitcoat, revealing a shoulder holster.

PEDRO: Tell him you're up for parole, that we're gonna move you to another cell in 24 hours.

MOLINA: Yes, sir.

WARDEN: And this is your last chance, so get going. You got 24 hours.

MOLINA: One thing, sir. You can't catch a fish without bait. I need more food. This time, sir, I prepared a list.

(Molina hands him a long list.)

(CUT TO:)

INT. CELL — NIGHT

Molina still sits on Valentin's bunk.

MOLINA: They'll probably move me to another cell in 24 hours. My lawyer says that's the procedure.

(Valentin turns away. Molina walks back to his own bunk.)

MOLINA: I don't want to get my hopes up too high. Do you want an apple?

VALENTIN: No, thanks. I guess I should be happy for you, but uh — I don't know.

MOLINA: Yes, all I wanted in life was to get out of here and take care of my mother. Nothing else mattered, but now that my wish might be —

VALENTIN: Be happy, dammit. I'd give anything to get out.

MOLINA: But is it fair?

VALENTIN: What?

MOLINA: That I always end up with nothing. That I don't have anything truly my own in life.

VALENTIN: You've got your mother.

MOLINA: Yes, but listen though. She's had a life and lived it. She had a husband and a son, but I'm still waiting.

VALENTIN: At least she's still alive.

MOLINA: But so am I. When is my life supposed to begin?
(*pause*)
When do I strike it lucky and have something for my own?

VALENTIN: (*approaches*) Right now. You just *got* lucky. Take advantage of it. You're getting out.

MOLINA: And do what? Hang out with my friends, a bunch of silly old queens like me? Tell a few jokes until I can't stand the sight of them, because they're a bunch of mirrors that send me running for my life? My life of waiting for nothing.

VALENTIN: Tell a movie. You'll feel better.
(*Curfew* BUZZER. *The dim light bulb goes out. Valentin moves to his bunk.*
Alone in the dark, Molina turns to the moonlit window and spins another web.)

MOLINA: Once upon a time, on a tropical island far away, there lived a strange woman.
(*pause*)
She wore a long gown of black lamé that fit her like a glove. But the poor thing, she was caught in a giant spider web that grew from her own body.
(CUT TO:)

EXT. TROPICAL BEACH — NIGHT (SPIDER MOVIE)

The masked SPIDER WOMAN *stands silhouetted against the moonlit ocean, waiting and waiting inside a huge silvery spider web.*
Gliding from the web, she moves across the sandy beach and slowly approaches the body of a MAN *washed onto her island shore.*

VOICE OF MOLINA: One day a shipwrecked man drifted onto the
beach.
(*She kneels in the sand beside him.* INSERT: *Valentin leans against
the cell wall, listening in the candlelight.*)
VOICE OF MOLINA: She fed him and cared for his wounds. She
nourished him with love and brought him back to life.
(*The Shipwrecked Man opens his eyes.*)
VOICE OF MOLINA: When he awoke, he gazed up at the Spider
Woman and saw a perfect tear-drop slide from under her
mask.
(CUT TO:)

Misty-eyed, Molina steps into the candlelight and approaches Valentin.
INSERT: *The Shipwrecked Man lifts his head for a closer look at the*
Spider Woman.

VOICE OF VALENTIN: Why is she crying?
   (Molina answers with a lump in his throat.)
MOLINA: I don't know. Why do you always need explanations?
   (sad sigh)
   Valentin, I'm tired. Tired of suffering. You're not the only
   one they've hurt. You don't know, I hurt so much inside.
VALENTIN: Where does it hurt you?
MOLINA: In my neck and shoulders. Why does the sadness
   always jam up in the same spot?
   (Valentin places a sympathetic hand on his shoulder. Molina
   tightens up and pulls away.)
MOLINA: Please. Don't touch me.
VALENTIN: Can't a friend even pat your back?
MOLINA: *(sits on bunk)* It only makes it worse.
VALENTIN: Why?
   (Molina, dropping his many masks, speaks with stark
   vulnerability.)
MOLINA: Because I've fallen in love with you.
   (pause)
   I'm sorry, Valentin, I wish it hadn't happened.
VALENTIN: *(looks away)* I understand.
   (looks back)
   Don't be ashamed.
   (Valentin moves to Molina's bunk and tentatively sits down.
   Molina, motionless, keeps looking away. Valentin clears his throat
   and says:)
VALENTIN: Can I touch you?
MOLINA: *(looking away)* If it doesn't disgust you.
   (pause)
   I'd like you to.
   (Valentin wraps a friendly arm around his shoulders. Molina
   shudders, then turns and looks apprehensively into his eyes.)
MOLINA: Can I touch your scar?

71

VALENTIN: (*shrugs*) Sure.

> (*Molina gently caresses the scar near Valentin's eyebrow, then rests his head on Valentin's chest and whispers:*)

MOLINA: Do what you want with me, because that's what I want.

> (*pause*)

If it doesn't disgust you.

VALENTIN: (*hesitant*) Okay.

> (*Molina trembles. Valentin holds him against his chest like a father comforting a child. Molina looks up and says:*)

MOLINA: You are so kind to me.

VALENTIN: No. You're the one who's kind.
(*Valentin straightens up and removes his shirt, then leans forward and blows out the candle.*
The cell is dark. The camera lingers on the candle-spark amid whisps of smoke.)
MOLINA (O.S.): Wait. I'm squeezed against the wall. That's better.
(*pause*)
No, wait. Let me lift my legs.
(*The spark fades. The screen is* BLACK.)
(CUT TO:)

INT. CELL — DAY

Molina, radiant, looks at the morning sunlight.

MOLINA: You know when I woke up, I put my hand to my eyebrow, to feel my scar like—
VALENTIN: You don't have one.
MOLINA: —like I wasn't me anymore. As if somehow I was you.
(*pause*)
Look, let's not talk about this. Let' s not talk about anything at all. Just for this morning I'm asking. Aren't you going to ask me why?
VALENTIN: Why?
MOLINA: Because I'm happy, I'm really happy, and I don't want to spoil it.
(*sad smile*)
The nicest thing about feeling happy is that you think you'll never feel unhappy again.
(CUT TO:)

INT. WARDEN'S OFFICE — DAY

Pedro, seething, leans into Molina's face.

PEDRO: You shit-face motherfuck. Talk!
(*Molina looks down in fear. The Warden wheels forward and motions Pedro away.*)

73

WARDEN: Let me handle this.

(*wheels closer*)

Look at me, Molina. What's the matter? You're afraid his group will kill you, is that it?

MOLINA: No sir. I *want* to help.

WARDEN: So what did he say?

MOLINA: Nothing. Wouldn't it be worse if I told you something that wasn't true?

WARDEN: I'll have to move you to another cell, Molina.

MOLINA: No sir, please. Don't do that. As long as I'm with him, there's still a chance that he might talk.

(*Pedro leans around the Warden into Molina's face.*)

PEDRO: You faggot piece of shit! You fell in love with that bastard.

WARDEN: Okay, Molina. You can go.

(*Molina stands up. The Warden reaches in his pocket.*)

WARDEN: Get your things ready. You're leaving today.

(*hands document*)

Here, the Ministry approved your parole.

(*Molina kisses the Warden's hand.*)

MOLINA: Thank you, sir.

WARDEN: And no more hanky-panky with the little boys.

MOLINA: Oh no, sir. I swear.

(*Molina leaves.*)

(CUT TO:)

INT. CELL — DAY

Molina pulls his mother's photo from the wall and packs his suitcase. Valentin stoops beside him.

VALENTIN: They, they would never suspect you. I mean really, there's no risk at all.

MOLINA: Sorry, I can't do it. I, uh, I'm just too afraid.

VALENTIN: All you have to do is give them a message. From any public phone.

MOLINA: No. No names, no phone numbers, nothing. I'm terrified of the police.

74

VALENTIN: Okay. I guess I shouldn't drag you into this.
   (*Valentin moves to the far corner. Molina watches him.*)
MOLINA: I swear, Valentin. My only desire is to stay here with
   you.
VALENTIN: Take care of yourself.
MOLINA: Valentin, I've only loved two people in my life. My
   mother and you.
VALENTIN: I'm gonna miss you, Molina
MOLINA: At least the movies.

VALENTIN: (*smiles*) Yeah, whenever I go to sleep, I'll probably be thinking of you and your crazy movies.

MOLINA: And whenever I see bonbons, I'll be thinking of you.
(*pause*)
Valentin, there's something I'd like to ask you, although we've done much more.
(*pause*)
A kiss.

VALENTIN: Okay. But first promise me something.

MOLINA: I told you, I can't. I'm so sorry.

VALENTIN: No, no, no.
(*approaches*)
Promise you'll never let anybody humiliate you again, that you'll make them respect you. Promise me you'll never let anybody exploit you again. Nobody has the right to do that to anybody.

MOLINA: (*deeply moved*)
I promise. Thank you.
(*pause*)
Valentin?

VALENTIN: What? The kiss?

MOLINA: No. The uhh. The phone number.
(*Valentin, overwhelmed, hugs him. Molina, surprised, returns the embrace.*)

VALENTIN: Wait a few days. Dial two times and hang up. The third time . . .
(*Valentin whispers in his ear. Molina nods twice. Their eyes meet. Valentin grips his shoulders and kisses him on the mouth. The Guard unlocks the door, then steps inside and says:*)

GUARD: Molina, let's go.
(*Molina picks up his suitcase and moves toward the door.*)

VALENTIN: Wait.
(*Valentin holds out the heart-shaped box. Molina, touched, takes it and looks deep into his eyes.*)

VALENTIN: Good luck, Molina.
(*Molina nods with a sad smile. The Guard pushes him outside.*)

GUARD: Come on.
(*The door is slammed shut on Valentin.*)
(CUT TO:)

EXT. PRISON COURTYARD — DAY

The Guard escorts Molina across the courtyard to the gate.

> (CUT TO:)

INT. CELL — DAY

Valentin, alone, paces the empty cell, then sits down and stares at Molina's bunk.

> (CUT TO:)

EXT. PRISON GATE — DAY

Molina crosses the busy street to a bus stop, then turns to the nearby counter of an open cafe.

MOLINA: A beer.
> (*The waiter uncaps a beer bottle.*)
> (CUT TO:)

INT. WARDEN'S OFFICE — DAY

Pedro opens the venetian blinds and watches Molina sipping beer at the bus stop. We HEAR *him typing a Secret Police report.*

VOICE OF PEDRO: Subject was granted a special parole by the Minister of Justice, on orders from the Department of Political Surveillance. The Department believes he will lead our agents to the cadre of Valentin Arregui.
> (*The bus arrives. Molina tosses his bottle in a trash can and climbs on board.*)
> (CUT TO:)

INT. BUS — DAY

Molina watches the passing city with sad and empty eyes.

> (CUT TO:)

INT. MOLINA'S APARTMENT — DAY

Molina opens the door, moves quietly down the hallway and sees her at the sewing machine, unspooling thread with the quiet precision of a spider.

MOLINA: —Mama.
MOTHER: (*surprised*) Ahhh.
    (*She hurries into his waiting arms. He wraps her in a warm embrace.*)
    (CUT TO:)

INT. CABARET — NIGHT

Molina, wearing a leopard pullover, crosses a smoke-filled cabaret to a table of MIDDLE-AGED HOMOSEXUALS. *They flatter him with campy flair.*

GROUP VOICES: —Luisa! So nice to see you!— You look great! Ten years younger, darling. Doesn't she?— The return of the Leopard Woman.
    (*Molina's transvestite friend Greta finishes a song on the small stage and approaches the microphone.*)
GRETA: (*rowdy applause*) Oh shut up, you bunch of faggots.
    (*indicates Molina*)
I'd like to welcome home a cherished sister who sacrificed Lord-knows-how-many precious nights to pay a stupid debt to a hypocritical society.
(*throws a kiss*)
This is for you, lovely Luisa.
(*He sings in a feminine voice. Molina, touched, nods.*)
(CUT TO:)

INT. MOLINA'S APARTMENT — NIGHT

Molina, motionless, sits in the bay window. His stark sad eyes gaze across the city lights at the prison on the dark horizon.

    (CUT TO:)

EXT. MOLINA'S APARTMENT — NIGHT

Pedro waits in a car parked in the shadows. His piercing eyes are fixed on Molina in the bay window. We HEAR *him file a police report.*

VOICE OF PEDRO: Surveillance reveals subject has not returned to work and almost never leaves home. He spends his evenings staring out the window for no apparent reason.
(CUT TO:)

INT. RESTAURANT — DAY

Molina sips coffee alone at a table. Gabriel approaches.

GABRIEL: You sure you won't eat something?
MOLINA: Just coffee.
GABRIEL: You wanna talk, Molina? Is something wrong?
MOLINA: No, I'm just not gonna see you for awhile. I'm going away.
GABRIEL: With another boy?
(*sad smile*)
That's good. Don't get arrested again. You're too old for it.
(CUT TO:)

INT. MOLINA'S APARTMENT — NIGHT

Molina sits with his arm around his frail mother. They are bathed in the blue radiance of a late movie on TV.

(CUT TO:)

INT. MOLINA'S BEDROOM — NIGHT

Molina slumps in bed in the robe he wore in prison. A red lamp illumines his poster of Rita Hayworth.
His sad eyes stare at the red box in his lap. His fingers trace the heart-shaped edges.

(CUT TO:)

INT. BAY WINDOW — NIGHT

Molina sits in the bay window with his head in his hands, then lifts his head and gazes across the rooftops at the distant prison.
Wearing a yellow satin jacket, he is dressed to go out but remains seated. Finally he sighs and moves to the door.

(CUT TO:)

INT. SUBWAY STATION — NIGHT

Molina enters an empty subway station, glances around and approaches a row of futuristic phones.
He dials twice and hangs up, then dials a third time and nervously brushes back his red-tinted hair.

MOLINA: I have a message from Valentin Arregui.
    (*short pause*)
    Yes, a pay phone.
    (*short pause*)
    Excuse me, is that really necessary?
    (*long pause*)
    Alright. I'll be wearing a red scarf.
    (CUT TO:)

INT. BANK — DAY

The BANK TELLER *hands Molina a thick wad of money.*

TELLER: You don't have to close your account. There's no
    penalty if you maintain a minimum balance of—
MOLINA: Thank you. Do you have an envelope please?
    (*Molina slips the money in the envelope and leaves.*)
    (CUT TO:)

EXT. PARK — DAY

Molina sits on a park bench with Greta and hands him the envelope.

MOLINA: This is for Mama. To take care of her while I'm gone. Please.

GRETA: All right, I'll handle it.

(*pause*)

Wherever you're going, it's probably for the best.

(CUT TO:)

INT. MOTHER'S BEDROOM — NIGHT

Molina tiptoes into his mother's bedroom and whispers:

MOLINA: Mama, you look so beautiful.

(*She is asleep. He gently kneels beside her.*)

MOLINA: You remember, Mama, when I was little and you used to come into my room to kiss me goodnight. I always pretended to be asleep, but I was always waiting for your kiss.

(*pause*)

Although you're sleeping now, I know you understand me. It's time for me to take care of my own life. You understand, don't you, Mama?

(*pause*)

Don't be sad.

(*He kisses her forehead.*)

(CUT TO:)

INT. MOLINA'S BEDROOM — DAY

Molina steps to his bedroom mirror and, expressionless, ties a red scarf around his neck. Rita Hayworth watches over his shoulder.

(CUT TO:)

EXT. CITY STREETS — DAY

Molina, tense, jockeys his way through a street jammed with pedestrians. Glancing up, he spots Pedro and three Secret Agents on an overpass.

*Frightened, Molina plunges into the crowd. Pedro sprints down the
overpass and barges through the crowd, his Agents right behind him.
Molina turns a corner into a shopping arcade and, hurrying, glances
back. He sees Pedro round the corner and stare into his eyes.
Molina desperately elbows through the shoppers. Pedro keeps a safe
distance.
Struggling, Molina weaves his way inside a dense cluster of pedestrians,
then darts down a narrow alley.
Pedro scans the four alleys. Molina is gone.*

PEDRO: Go that way. Hurry.
> (*The Agents split into two groups and go the wrong way.*)
> (CUT TO:)

EXT. CATHEDRAL SQUARE — DAY

*Molina steps from an alley into an open square. Fingering his red scarf,
he searches the crowd for Secret Police.
Relieved, he crosses the square to the cathedral and stops beside a
BEGGAR playing an accordion. Pretending to listen, he scrutinizes the
street and nervously taps his teeth.
A white taxi slowly approaches the cathedral steps. The YOUNG
WOMAN beside the driver nervously eyes Molina.
He hesitantly stoops down and sees a pistol half-hidden by a newspaper
on her lap. She leans out the window.*

LYDIA: — Who are you?
MOLINA: I have a message from Valentin. Are you Lydia?
LYDIA: Yes, get in. Quick.
> (*Molina reaches for the door handle.*)
PEDRO: Get 'em!
> (*Suddenly an Agent slams Molina aside and thrusts a revolver in
> the window. Lydia rapid-fires two shots and blasts the Agent to
> the pavement.
> The taxi roars away. Molina runs. Pedro and two Agents bolt
> forward, firing at the taxi careening through the terrified crowd.
> Turning, Pedro sprints after Molina disappearing into a dark*

alley. The two Agents follow at top speed, firing warning shots in the air.)
(CUT TO:)

EXT. PLAZA — DAY

Molina, gasping, races along the dark alley toward the sunlit plaza across a busy avenue.
Pedro barrels around the corner with his automatic pistol and charges down the alley. Bystanders run for cover.

PEDRO: Molina! Stop!
(Molina rushes toward the plaza when, suddenly, the white taxi skids to a stop on the avenue directly ahead. Lydia rapid-fires three shots out the window.
Molina, twisted sideways, grabs his bleeding chest. The taxi screeches away. Molina lurches across the avenue into the plaza. Bystanders scream and scatter. Pedro reaches the corner and fires at the fleeing taxi, then aims at Molina and strides into the plaza. Molina, clutching his blood-stained shirt, staggers into a flock of pigeons. Agents surround him with aimed handguns. Molina turns and faces them, then drops to his knees.
The pigeons scatter. Pedro motions to an Agent.)
PEDRO: Get the car. Move, hurry.
(The Agent runs. Pedro steps forward and slowly circles behind Molina, then jams the automatic against the back of his head and frisks him.
The car pulls up. Pedro jerks Molina to his feet.)
PEDRO: Get up. Move! Get in the car.
(Pedro hurls Molina into the backseat, climbs in and slams the door. The car speeds away.)
(CUT TO:)

INT. PEDRO'S CAR — DAY

Molina lies stretched out on the backseat. Pedro straddles his waist and sticks the automatic in his face.

PEDRO: The number. Tell me the phone number and you go to the hospital.

(*Molina spits up foamy blood, then calmly gazes at Pedro.*)

PEDRO: Talk! You fucking fag!

(*Molina's eyes slowly close. His head slumps sideways.*)

(CUT TO:)

EXT. SLUM — DAY

The car turns off a busy street into a shanty-town slum and stops beside a pile of garbage.
Pedro drags Molina's body from the backseat and dumps it on the garbage.

VOICE OF PEDRO: Subject was shot to death by the extremists. His recent activities, such as closing his bank account, suggest that he planned to escape with them. Also, the way he was shot seems to indicate he had agreed, if necessary, to be eliminated by them.

(*pause*)

In any case, it appears he was more deeply involved than we suspected.

(CUT TO:)

INT. PRISON INFIRMARY — DAY

Valentin, dying, lies on a cot. His face is swollen with bloody bruises.
His chest is disfigured by electric burns.
A prison INTERN *takes out a hypodermic needle.*

INTERN: This is morphine. So you can get some rest, okay?

(*Valentin nods feebly. The Intern injects the needle.*)

INTERN: My God, the way they worked you over.

(*removes needle*)

Just don't tell about this or I'll lose my job. Count to forty and you'll be asleep.

(*Valentin takes two deep breaths and falls sound asleep. A*

woman's dream-like hand slowly reaches out and touches his
wrist.)

VOICE OF VALENTIN: . . . Marta . . .
(Valentin turns in his sleep and sees the beaming smile of his love.
Marta, vibrant in a pure white dress, caresses his battered head and
tenderly tugs him to his feet.)

MARTA: Come, Valentin, come with me. Don't be afraid. You
won't wake up in the cell.
(CUT TO:)

EXT. PRISON COURTYARD — DAY (DREAM)

Running hand-in-hand, Marta leads Valentin across the dark courtyard
toward the gate. The guards and prisoners cannot see them. Valentin,
bleeding, stops and looks back.

VOICE OF VALENTIN: — What about Molina?
VOICE OF MARTA: Come, my love. Only he knows if he died
happy or sad.
(She takes his hand and opens the prison gate, revealing a burst of
sunlight.)
(CUT TO:)

EXT. TROPICAL ISLAND — DAY (DREAM)

Smiling in the sunshine, they run toward the ocean across a sandy beach
— the same beach in Molina's movie about the Spider Woman.
Valentin, radiant, has no scars or wounds. Stopping at the shoreline, he
brushes back her hair and looks into her eyes.

VOICE OF VALENTIN: I love you so much. That's the one thing I
never said, because I was afraid of losing you forever.
(They kiss warmly. Marta caresses his healed face and looks into
his loving eyes.)
VOICE OF MARTA: That can never happen now. This dream is
short, but this dream is happy.
(Holding hands, they wade into the water and climb into a wooden
rowboat. Taking the oars, Valentin rows farther and farther
toward the sparkling horizon.)